Nationalism & Identity

The Danes and their neighbours

Denmark is a Scandinavian country, but not a very Scandinavian country. It has no midnight sun, no ski-jumps and no reindeer.

Outsiders tend to think of the Scandinavians as all the same, but they are not. The Norwegians are like the Scots; a hardy mountain folk. Swedes are the Prussians of the North; they stand up straight, dress alike and do what they are told. The Danes are more relaxed and easy-going. They sit down: it increases the chances of everyone seeing eye to eye.

> **❝ Denmark is a Scandinavian country, but not a very Scandinavian country. ❞**

The differences between these three peoples are best understood by considering the most famous writer of each country: Ibsen for Norway, Strindberg for Sweden and Hans Christian Andersen for Denmark,

They are also reflected in attitudes to alcohol. In Denmark alcohol is freely available and relatively cheap. In Norway and Sweden alcohol is pricey and sales are under state control; a licence is needed not just to sell alcohol, but to buy it. This is good news for Copenhagen bars, which do a lively trade selling Danish firewater to thirsty Swedes and Norwegians on the razzle. No Swedish politician would ever be seen with a beer in his hand, but Danes are happy to see

1

Danish politicians not only holding a beer, but drinking it – although they baulk at footing the bill if it's done 'outside office hours'.

The Danes think of their neighbours as they would members of their family. Denmark is the baby sister whose idea of fun occasionally shocks. The other Scandinavian countries are of course brothers. Finland is the one who is moody, unpredictable and possibly autistic. Norway is accepted as equal, perhaps even slightly envied for its oil wealth, natural beauty and exclusivity. Sweden is the boring older brother who thinks he knows best, is well dressed, well behaved and infuriatingly politically correct. However, Sweden offers lower tax, cheaper housing and luxury cars at giveaway prices compared with Denmark. Younger Danes have a sneaking admiration for the Swedes that they try to keep hidden.

> **❝ The Danes think of their neighbours as they would members of their family. Denmark is the baby sister whose idea of fun occasionally shocks. ❞**

The Swedish countryside is much admired and many Danes holiday in Sweden, but they feel somehow that Swedes don't deserve their wonderful surroundings. In Danish eyes Sweden is a cultural and human desert. There are rules about everything and you need a second mortgage to stand a round of drinks. Both countries have fines for dogs fouling the pavement, but in Sweden you actually get caught.

In the spirit of New Europe, Danes try very hard to like the Germans, but it's hard work not to bite the hand that feeds them. Danes are convinced that the Germans are trying to take over Europe, cunningly disguised as tourists. They are intensely concerned that the *pølse tyskere* (sausage Germans) will buy Jutland as soon as they get the chance and turn it into a windsurfing centre. Germans regularly fall asleep on their sailboards and have to be fished out of the North Sea halfway to Grimsby by the long-suffering Danish air-sea rescue service. All the summer houses are rented out to Germans, there are even German editions of local newspapers, and LEGOLAND, complete with a part of the Rhine Valley, is filled to the brim with Germans determined to enjoy themselves. However, Germans are more acceptable if they buy plenty of Danish products. They are also partially forgiven for being German if they employ Danes in their businesses.

> **The Danes attribute their success to having all the virtues of their neighbours and none of their vices.**

Inflation in Denmark is negligible, the economy is strong and technological development is world-class – not bad for a country with a population roughly that of South London. The Danes attribute this success to their having all the virtues of their neighbours and none of their vices. They share the Germans' methodical attention to detail and the Swedes' egalitarianism

3

and level-headedness. Gone is the plodding, constipated German imagination (or lack of it) and the dreary Swedish party-pooping pedantry. According to the Danes, what's left is a unique mixture of conscientiousness and informality that makes Danish overseas travellers breathe a sigh of relief when they cross the border home.

High fliers

The Danes fly their flag with pride. The red and white '*Dannebrog*' against a clear blue sky is enough to bring a tear to their eyes. Rural inhabitants invariably have their own flag pole set squarely in the middle of their garden. Town dwellers rent an allotment and plant a pole along with their broad-leaved parsley. Both have lists of dates magneted to the fridge giving details of when to 'let rip' – public holidays, festivals, state visits, their own birthdays, anniversaries, etc., and town 'fêtes' when flags line the main street to remind everyone that the local shops stay open late that night.

> **Danes who cannot fly flags out of doors have mini flagpoles as part of their table decoration for high days and holidays.**

Danes who cannot fly flags out of doors have mini flagpoles as part of their table decoration for high days and holidays, and even fly the flag on cocktail sticks. Shops and advertisers use the flag to promote their goods, and Danish football fans were the first to paint their faces with their national flag.

There is nothing threatening about this nationalism. As a nation, the Danes have not been a threat to anyone for hundreds of years.

How they see others

The rugged individualism of American society is at odds with the importance which Danes attach to social cohesion. Americans are seen as an essential ally and the scientific research they generate is admired, but if a situation is approaching unacceptable levels, for example, Danish children are being fed too much fast food, a Danish academic of some description will appear on the news proclaiming that Denmark is hurtling towards an '*amerikansk tilstand*' (an American state of affairs).

> **66 The rugged individualism of American society is at odds with the importance which Danes attach to social cohesion. 99**

The British are regarded as class-ridden with Dickensian social values, a view supported by costume dramas shown on television. This does not prevent Danes from showing great enthusiasm for the English language, English pop music and league football. Though deeply censorious of the Germans and pitying of the Swedes, the Danes are angels of patience and tolerance when it comes to the English. The drunken buffoonery of English football fans is met with smiles of understanding. The sight of an English football fan halfway up a lamppost swilling beer from the anus of an inflatable rubber pig caused little more than some shaking of heads. A German or a Swede would have been arrested and heavily fined.

> **There are really only two things that Danes may envy other nations: one is warm winters, and the other is a beautiful language.**

The Danes look on the outside world confident that they may not have achieved a perfect society, but they are closer to it than most other people. There are really only two things that Danes may envy other nations: one is warm winters, and the other is a beautiful language.

How they see themselves

Efficient, environmentally conscious and generous to those less fortunate outside their national borders are how most Danes see themselves. However, behind this idyllic description lurks the Danish tax man, '*skattefar*' (tax daddy), wielding more power than George Orwell's Big Brother.

The substantial taxes needed to support the well-developed welfare system (about 50%) are chalking up an ever-widening distinction between those who work and those who don't. Scratch the surface and you find that the Danes' image of themselves varies a great deal. At one extreme there are self-employed Danes who see themselves as freedom fighters manacled to an interfering state. For them, hours of extra paperwork mean that a working day often stretches into the night, and 'black work' (moonlighting) is a national sport. At the other extreme, more and more Danes are languishing on one of the highest unemployment benefits in Europe. The majority of the working population jogs along on the verge of Utopia, somewhere between the two.

The tax situation might explain the Danes' love of a good deal. Haggling is not unusual and impromptu flea markets are

> **66 Danes know with 100% certainty that Denmark is the best country in the world. 99**

common. Non-money transactions are also popular. 'I'll paint your windows if you update my website' (Copenhagen). 'I'll swap you a pig for your trailer' (Jutland). It's another way of diddling the taxman.

Taxes aside, Danes know with 100% certainty that Denmark is the best country in the world. To debate this immutable truth is evidence of mental instability. Denmark consistently takes top place in the United Nations World Happiness reports – a fact that is only surprising to non-Danes. Deep down Danes believe that being Danish is a privilege and makes them special. They say that if Scandinavia is a bowl of rice pudding, Denmark is the '*smørhul*' – the golden hollow in the middle, full of melted butter. Ask them why, however, and they are unlikely to be able to string together enough positive adjectives to convince you. Sentences containing more than two such words prompt most Danes' innate 'anti-brag' filter to kick in. Positive words used by youngsters to mean 'cool' include *fedt* (fat) and *sej* (tough), both of which can be applied to bacon.

> **66 The Danes' mission in life is to help the rest of the world to see just how wonderful Denmark is. 99**

The Danes' mission in life is to help the rest of the world to see just how wonderful Denmark is. They feel sorry for all the poor souls who aren't Danish, have never visited their country, or otherwise live in heathen ignorance of their land of milk and honey. Even their closest neighbours remain in the dark. For instance, efforts to rebrand the nearby Swedish region of Skåne as 'Greater Copenhagen' (which could extend the Danish capital while bringing economic benefit to that part of Sweden) have so far met with resistance. Meanwhile, as they cannot bring themselves to boast about how fantastically lucky they are, they use an inordinate amount of time and energy trying to get others to see the light.

How they see other Danes

Even a country as small as Denmark has strong regional differences. Copenhageners make great show of not being able to understand some of the thicker regional accents in Jutland and regard travelling there with foreboding. For them it's full of scowling, muscle-bound yokels itching to put the city slickers in their place. Jutlanders are also seen as rural masters of understatement. According to popular belief, the Jutlander rarely says anything downright positive, for example when asked if he wants coffee, he doesn't say 'Yes', he says 'I wouldn't say no'.

Jutlanders see Copenhageners as a bunch of lily-livered, silver-tongued fops who like nothing better than doing them an injustice. They claim they are 'not as bad as all that'. In fact, all Danes have a better opinion of themselves than they allow themselves to express.

How others see them

The Danes are seen as the epitome of good order and good sense. They are not very excitable or romantic, they have neat painted houses set in neat countryside and they're good at business – a bit like the Swiss, but without the mountains.

Their language is unlearnable, their cultural identity elusive, but once their occasional childlike candour is forgiven, everyone likes the Danes. It is difficult not to like the creators of LEGO, the producers of so much bacon and butter, and the brewers of (probably) the best beer in the world.

Character

Today's Danes are a peaceable people. The only helmeted warriors left are bikers. When the Danish Vikings colonised the British Isles, they must have taken with them all the most unruly elements. Ever since, the British have behaved like Vikings, while the Danes have constructed a modern liberal welfare state where everyone is cared for, and their football fans are generally models of propriety.

> **66 Today's Danes are a peaceable people. The only helmeted warriors left are bikers. 99**

Denmark is a land of modesty and moderation. This is largely a consequence of the Danes' sense of social responsibility. The touchstone of any activity or point of view is whether it is *samfundsrelevant*, that is, socially useful.

Indoctrination concerning the individual's responsibility begins early. Danish children are brought up with stories featuring Teddy, Chicken and Duckling. Teddy and his friends regularly face the conflict of individual needs versus the common good. The peak-rated televised version shows the characters having a witty and wonderful time, eating, drinking, dancing and laughing, so the young get the idea that social responsibility does not have to be onerous. Adults are still enchanted, not so much by the message as by the sight of three grown-ups wearing fur costumes, huffing and puffing about in a forest while trying to sing and avoid heatstroke in unison.

However, to really get to grips with the Danish character one needs to understand two words: *hygge* and *Janteloven*.

Hygge

A love of or need for *hygge* is an important part of the Danish psyche. *Hygge* is usually inadequately translated as 'cosiness'. This is too simplistic: cosiness relates to physical surroundings – a jersey can be cosy, or a warm bed – whereas *hygge* has more to do with people's behaviour towards each other. It is the art of creating intimacy: a sense of comradeship, conviviality, and contentment rolled into one.

> **66** *Hygge* **is the art of creating intimacy: a sense of comradeship, conviviality, and contentment rolled into one. 99**

Friends meeting in the street might say that it has been *hyggeligt* to see each other, and someone who is fun to be with can be called a *hyggelig fyr*, when he would hardly be described as a 'cosy fellow'. The truly emotive depth of the word *hyggelig* is best captured by considering its opposite, *uhyggeligt*, which means anything from cheerless through sinister to downright shocking and grisly.

To have a *hyggelig* time is social nirvana in Denmark.

11

Candlelight is used to encourage a *hyggelig* atmosphere. The Danes love candles and use them everywhere, both in public at cafés, bars, restaurants and offices, and in the home where they are put out along with the cat last thing at night. The dim lighting helps to soften the clean, uncluttered surfaces and uncompromising white walls that are typical features of Danish living rooms. The ideal is to have a Christiania *kakkelovn* (antique stove) or an open fireplace and feel the warmth from its *hyggelige* glow.

> 66 The core of *Jante's* laws is that anyone who sets himself above the rest of the group will be knocked off his perch. 99

Achieving *hygge* generally involves being with friends and family, and eating and drinking. Older Danes are horrified by youngsters who *hygger* themselves alone on the sofa with a DVD and a family-sized bag of sweets.

Janteloven

Whenever there is a group of Danes at work, at the sports club, even when supposedly letting off steam, group pressure is evident. Danes even applaud in unison. This code of conformity was first put into words by Aksel Sandemose, a Dane who was so weary of its effects on the people in the area of Jutland where he lived that he broke ranks and moved to Norway.

He then wrote a book about life in a fictional Danish town called Jante, which was governed by laws (*loven* = the law) that described the deep-rooted social attitudes he had observed.

The core of Jante's laws is that anyone who sets himself above the rest of the group will be knocked off his perch. There are ten commandments, so similar in nature that one or two are enough to put any would-be Danish individualist squarely in his place:

1. You must not believe that you are anybody.
2. You must not believe you are as important as us.
3. You must not believe you are cleverer than us.
4. You must not deceive yourself that you are better than us.
5. You must not believe that you know more than us.
6. You must not believe that you are more than us.
7. You must not think that you are good at anything.
8. You must not laugh at us.
9. You must not think that anyone cares about you.
10. You must not believe that you can teach us anything.

The code is so ingrained in the Danish mind that a good many believe it originated in the Middle Ages. In fact, it was written in 1933. Though created in irony, these codes have become crystallised in a set of modern-day values every bit as entrenched as the fictitious ones:

1. You must believe everybody is somebody.

2. You must believe everyone is as important as everyone else.

3. You may be cleverer, but that does not make you a better person.

4. You must believe everyone is as good as you.

5. You must believe everyone knows something worth knowing.

6. You must think of everyone as your equal.

7. You must believe everyone can be good at something.

8. You must not laugh at others.

9. You must think everyone is equally worth caring about.

10. You can learn something from everyone.

Every now and again the media focuses on the question of whether *Janteloven* still exists. Although many people say it no longer does, Danish behaviour proves that *Janteloven* still casts a long shadow. For example, if an author is naïve enough to give a fellow Dane a manuscript of a story he is writing, the Dane will read it, give it back and say, 'I read another book about the same subject last year.' Park a brand new car in the driveway and the questions begin. 'Is it a company car?', 'Bought it second-hand, did you?', 'Someone leave you a little legacy then?'

It's a foolish Dane who bursts in on his friends,

brimming with excitement and announcing 'Guess what, I've just won a contract to sell a new kind of water softener!' The right way to handle this is to walk in looking tired and announce that you've just come back from a really tough meeting; then wait to have the good news drawn out of you like a rotten tooth.

The spirit of *Janteloven* makes life difficult for Danish copywriters. Companies dislike drawing attention to their achievements, or pointing out their strengths, preferring to distance the accomplishments from the people who achieved them. This results in a palatably modest, or even humble, tone.

One word that copywriters can use in abundance is '*mulighed*', often modestly translated as 'possibility' but closer to 'opportunity'. From this people are encouraged to think that Denmark is a land of opportunity with Danish products opening up opportunities left, right and centre.

Some do their best to point out the negative impact of this attention phobia. However, en masse the Danes are content

66 Companies dislike drawing attention to their achievements or pointing out their strengths. 99

to remain firmly grouped together on the ground, happy to brood the fate and await the downfall of those who dare to fly solo. As the Danish maxim goes: 'The higher up a monkey climbs, the more you see of its bottom.'

Attitudes & Values

Danish society is consensual rather than adversarial. It's a small country so you have to be careful what you do – and who you do it with. The political and legal systems aim at finding agreement rather than disagreement. In Denmark 'alternative' views are mainstream.

> **❝ The high degree of social conformity means that all right-thinking people end up with more or less the same opinions. ❞**

Danes try to see the other person's point of view, even though the divorce statistics may suggest that consensus is not always easy to achieve. While it is a liberal society, the high degree of social conformity means that all right-thinking people end up with more or less the same opinions. Differences are more a matter of degree than of principle.

Co-operation

Danes co-operate. LEGO derives from the Danish words *leg godt* which means 'play well', and this is just what the Danes are good at. If they can curb their inclination for honesty, they get along well with other people. The ability to co-operate is seen as an admirable quality, worth striving for in its own right. In any brochure translated for the world market the word 'co-operation' will appear at least three times per page along with a generous sprinkling of 'joint ventures'. In its heyday, even Christiania – an ecological hippy heaven established in an old military barracks in Copenhagen, with rain-water washing machines, solar panels and humus toilets – had joint, common and shared goals, committees, clubs, and a state-approved local area development plan.

The Danes co-operate not only with their colleagues but also with competitors because working together is regarded as enlightened self-interest. It is an attitude which depends on everyone sharing the same values. Meetings are inevitable, but seldom interminable.

> **66 The ability to co-operate is seen as an admirable quality, worth striving for in its own right. 99**

On a national level, important constitutional issues are decided by referenda. These are preceded by plenty of long, involved political debates broadcast at peak television viewing times. Online film streaming services look forward to them even if no-one else does.

High standards

Danes expect high standards in the goods and services they buy. They expect the trains to run on time, the streets to be clean and the tradespeople to know their business, which they do. In a restaurant, Danes are not afraid to complain if things are not to their taste, and the complaint is made without bitterness and received without rancour. The fact that they expect things to be done with *omhu* (care), and do not accept bad service or shoddy goods uncomplainingly, helps to maintain their high standards.

This focus on quality is maintained across the board. A front-page newspaper article told of a gentleman who had visited a 'lady of the night' and had subsequently reported her to the police for 'failing to supply the desired outcome'. The police duly investigated the matter but decided to drop the case when they discovered that the gentleman had been exceedingly drunk at the time and the lady in question had put in an hour's overtime in her efforts to satisfy her customer.

> **66 Danes expect things to be done with *omhu* (care), and do not accept bad service or shoddy goods uncomplainingly. 99**

Healthy living

In general, the Danes are very aware of what they put into themselves, although organic products are much more prevalent in the capital than in Jutland, where the locals tend to question the sanity of anyone willingly paying extra for anything. It's *pjat* (frivolous nonsense) and smacks of city slickness.

For those who care, foods that are 'natural' and

high in fibre are necessarily good; any additive of any kind is necessarily bad. Sugar is considered particularly heinous. One dentist's waiting room has half-litre fizzy-drink bottles hung up by the neck, displaying 32 lumps of sugar as a warning about the contents. Salt, however, seems to have weathered the storm of public antipathy. It has always been a common preservative in any Danish household. Salt the bacon. Salt the herring. Salt the liquorice. Salt the popcorn. Salt the cycle paths...

There is a general attitude that if vitamins are good, more vitamins are better. However, nothing keeps the Danes from enjoying beer, cakes, butter, cheese, hot dogs from the *pølsevogn* (sausage stand), chocolate and cola. Nor from exporting Danish salami which is such a bright pink, it looks radioactive.

Healthy living includes keeping fit and a lot of Danes attend exercise classes. Every town has its well-equipped sports hall and football pitch.

> **66 Salt has always been a common preservative in any Danish household. Salt the bacon. Salt the herring. Salt the liquorice. Salt the cycle paths... 99**

Visitors should be prepared for a shock at the swimming pool where there are compulsory open-plan showers and you have to shower before and after your swim. It's not only hard to keep your 'privates' from becoming public, but large signs show parts of the body targeted in red for an extra hard scrub.

Environmental concern

The Danes consider themselves leaders in environmental responsibility. Environmental awareness is a 'must' rather than a virtue, unless you're a Jutland farmer, in which case it's a legal requirement forced on you by meddling bureaucrats. To be *miljøvenlig* ('environmentally friendly') is highly socially responsible and is viewed as part of healthy living. As a result, they sort out their rubbish. They sort out their waste water. They sort out anyone caught dumping in the sea off their wonderful blue-flag, sandy beaches. They take the lead in the use of ozone-friendly chemicals, biodegradable plastics, and minimal packaging. Pollution is frowned upon. The country's farmers are regularly blamed for over-liberal use of pesticides ruining the groundwater and fjords.

> ❝ To be *miljøvenlig* ('environmentally friendly') is highly socially responsible and is viewed as part of healthy living. ❞

Some power stations are designed and built to run on waste materials. The use of sustainable energy sources such as solar energy, geothermal energy and wind turbines is encouraged by state subsidies. As the wind turbine manufacturer Vestas is a Danish company, many wind farms – forests of wind generators – are humming into action.

Well over half of Danish houses are supplied with hot water and central heating via well-insulated underground pipes from big, shared boilers. This district heating is much more efficient than each house having its own. Heat conservation has long been built-in, with houses having double or even triple glazing, cellars, and cavity and roof insulation as standard. The Danes consider conserving heat and electricity a social duty. Besides, in a landscape of white, a roof with melted snow sticks out like a sore thumb.

Local rubbish tips ('Recycling Stations') often have Scout containers for jumble sale items. Most bottles carry a deposit which is redeemed when you return them for re-cycling. This practice was objected to by the European Commission as putting imported drinks at a disadvantage. Naturally the Danes argued that the planet was more important than European competition law. For most Danes one of the advantages of belonging to international organisations like the EU is to help solve environmental problems, not cause them. Danish Euro scepticism is based on a concern that Denmark will have to lower its standards on the environment, as well as product safety and food hygiene. The fact that the word 'Euro' is like '*uro*' (meaning trouble, unrest, disquiet and concern) doesn't help either.

> **66 Danish Euro scepticism is based on a concern that Denmark will have to lower its standards. 99**

Consumers are selective and well informed. They react as one to political issues and take pride in, for instance, boycotting oil companies and bullying dairy monopolies. Fur is a rather more sensitive issue. Denmark has an old and very respected fur trade, and even in relatively mild winters, women of all ages emerge on the streets wearing sealskin coats. If questioned, they earnestly explain that they are helping to uphold a traditional native craft which forms the base of the Greenland economy.

Religion

Religious devotion is a regional phenomenon in Denmark. An austere fundamentalism flourishes on the west coast of Jutland in the areas where fishing was the traditional occupation. Life was hard and short and this was, and still is, reflected in the religious beliefs of these communities.

> **66 Everybody pays church tax unless they specifically opt out, which few do. 99**

The official religion of the Danes is Lutheran. Everybody pays church tax unless they specifically opt out, which relatively few do. Since they retain their church membership by paying church taxes, most Danes use it at least four times during their lives, for their baptism, confirmation, marriage (at least once) and funeral.

Confirmations are the most popular religious ritual. Many are more like weddings than weddings themselves with present lists, table plans, elaborate white dresses for the girls and smart outfits for the boys. There is even a kind of honeymoon called a 'Blue Monday', which is a day off school for the individuals concerned.

Even if religion is not involved, similarly lavish 'non-firmation' parties are held. Either way, the adolescent becomes the embarrassed

> 66 Confirmations are the most popular religious ritual. Many are more like weddings than weddings themselves. 99

centre of attention, both as the squirming object of speeches by maudlin uncles and tearfully cheerful aunts, and the mortified subject of intimate verses composed and sung by his or her family and friends. Only after this ritual humiliation can the recipient scuttle off to review the day's takings.

The lives of Danes are also influenced by a rather more sombre song-writer, N.F.S. Grundtvig, a priest (and son of a priest), who died in 1872 at the age of nearly 90. He wrote over 1,400 hymns, dredging up old Nordic words and bolting them together almost regardless of meaning. Though appreciated by a few, such orotundities may help explain the generally low church attendance.

Grundtvig described Denmark as the country where 'few have too much and fewer too little'. His hymns, and the Folk High Schools he established are his lasting legacy. When introduced, the schools gave education to tens of thousands of working people including farm workers.

Grundtvig was charismatic, little concerned with orthodox theology and a thorn in the side of the church authorities. However, the unorthodox views of yesterday can today become orthodox; he lived so long and said so many different and contradictory things that it is possible for people of widely differing views to call themselves 'Grundtvigian'. Grundtvigianism, rather like Hinduism, embraces a variety of beliefs.

Happy Families

The Danes love getting married, but Danish marriages lack the famous 'clutching power' of the LEGO brick: Denmark has one of the highest divorce rates in Europe. Marriage can be a necessary preliminary to divorce. Couples will often cohabit for a long time in what are called 'paperless' marriages and will then formalise the arrangement before getting divorced. It is as if formalising a stable arrangement destabilises it.

> **66 Danish marriages lack the famous 'clutching power' of the LEGO brick. 99**

Denmark was the first country in Europe to allow a form of marriage for homosexuals, and permits same-sex marriages in church. This reflects the generally

24

liberal attitude that allows people to lead their lives as they choose, as long as they don't bother others. No-one twitches an eyebrow at those who choose to share their morning newspaper prior to marriage, and a couple's children will often attend their wedding.

Worldwide, Danes are seeded high in fertility circles. Rules regarding privacy for Danish sperm donors are ensuring a global comeback for the Viking gene pool. As it's a handy way for students to top up their income, the sperm banks are never short of deposits.

At home, a high proportion of babies are born to unmarried parents. This is not to say that babies born to unmarried parents are born outside a stable relationship, nor that,

> **66 Rules regarding privacy for Danish sperm donors are ensuring a global comeback for the Viking gene pool. 99**

given the high divorce rate, babies born to married parents are born within a stable relationship. In fact, it makes little or no difference to the children whether the parents are married or not. Whatever their relationship or its stability, most Danish children spend the majority of their waking hours being brought up by someone else. The Friday evening train service between Copenhagen and Jutland that carries children to and fro between parents who have moved to opposite ends of the country is nicknamed the divorce express.

Share care

Most parents go out to work. The high cost of living coupled with high taxation means they can't afford not to. Fortunately, there is widespread provision of maternity and paternity leave, crèches, nursery schools, childcare centres, and so on. All this leaves women equally free to continue their studies or pursue a meaningful, socially relevant career after they have become parents, and because of the back-up systems there is little excuse not to.

In many areas, housing estates are like ghost towns during the working day – except for some harassed adults shepherding long crocodiles of small children to and from local places of interest. King-size prams with two small occupants and one or two hangers-on also feature in the street scene. The poor women

66 All around you in the semi-darkness are the sounds of the gentle hicks and guzzlings of babies breast-feeding. 99

pushing what can amount to 80lbs of weight are not the victims of over-effective fertility treatment programmes. They are council-approved 'daycare mummies'.

'Baby bio' at some cinemas is more for mothers than their babies. Liberated mums time their babies' naps just right, park their prams in the foyer, collect a numbered ticket and go in to watch the film. They might not hear much of it though because every so often a head pops round the door and calls 'Number 6 your child is up', and all around you in the semi-darkness are the sounds of the gentle hicks and guzzlings of babies breast-feeding.

Children are placed in daycare institutions from the age of about a year. Later on, other daycare institutions take over at the end of the school day, where children entertain themselves until their parents arrive to collect them. As a result, during the week they get a homogenised upbringing provided by trained pedagogues, while at the weekends their parents (trying to balance the conflicting demands of work and family) are left squeezing a week's worth of love and affection into two days, plus the chaotic hour before the evening meal is served (*ulvetimen* = 'the wolves' hour').

> **66 Anti-social behaviour is verbally discouraged by whichever responsible adult is closest. 99**

Parental discipline is liberal. Good social behaviour is exhorted. Anti-social behaviour is verbally discouraged by whichever responsible adult is closest. Striking a child is illegal. Conflicts are normally nipped firmly in the bud before they escalate past the 'My Dads are bigger than your Dads*' stage.

---

*With the number of changes of partners there is a plurality of Mums and Dads – all except the natural ones being referred to as '*pap*' (cardboard) figures.

The elderly

Elderly Danes are independent and have lives of their own. Their *'Mimrekort'* ('dodderers' card') gives them cheap access to public transport, theatres, cinemas, museums, and evening classes in the daytime. Add to this daycare centres and home helps, and as long as the old stay healthy and alert, life can be fun.

Working mothers with offspring too sick to attend school are lucky if granny is available for babysitting. This explains the *'mormor ordning'* (grandma scheme) advertised in some kindergartens. Parents pay to sign up their children for the scheme and then kindly old ladies help out as granny stand-ins.

When they get too old or frail to look after themselves, grannies and grandads are shuffled off to suitably *hyggelige* old folks homes. Ordinary family housing is not designed for extended families. Also, with changing patterns of marriage, what obligation does someone have to look after his or her stepmother's second husband, or his third wife? People have enough to do sorting out pillow cases for their stepchildren without coping with their stepchildren's stepgrandparents.

Family names

The Danes take naming their children very seriously. Though they have a few names in mind before the

28

birth, parents often wait until the baby's personality begins to show before registering their final choice.

Most Danish surnames end in -sen, for example, Hansen ('Hans's son'). Surnames only became general about the middle of the 19th century. Until then if Hans had a son and called him Jens, he would be known as Jens Hansen. If Jens Hansen then had a son, and called him Hans, he would be called Hans Jensen. At some point it became customary for people to stick with the family name they had, and pass it on to their children. This is why many Danish surnames are so similar, Jensen, Hansen, Larsen, Nielsen.

> **Many women keep their maiden names in marriage, which enables them to retain their identity in cases of serial monogamy.**

Many women keep their maiden names in marriage, which enables them to retain their identity in cases of serial monogamy. Children inherit these double-barrelled names. If they meet a double-barrelled partner, they then have the choice of four surnames. This is easier than it sounds when two are likely to be Jensen or Hansen.

The fabric of society

Dress codes exist, but are situation-specific. Children do not wear school uniform, but they don't need to because from the age of six months they are dressed alike anyway. For comfort, and the convenience of the child-minder, clothing is index-linked to the weather forecast. By the time children start school, parents are fully aware of the advantages of investing in practical, washable, 100% waterproof, thermal, wool-lined garments that fasten with Velcro tapes. This rather narrows down the field of choice. Needless to say, nametapes are also obligatory – forenames included. Hold up a stray item and call out 'A. Jensen' and a forest of little hands shoots up.

In later life, dress codes can become more subtle. Once again, integration is the key. A female computer engineer must be careful not to look too smart or she could be mistaken for a secretary. A building consultant must look casual enough to be regarded by the labourers as one of the team, but smart enough to represent management.

> **A building consultant must look casual enough to be regarded by the labourers as one of the team, but smart enough to represent management.**

Though a class system as such does not exist, colour coding is widespread in Denmark. Gardeners wear green or brown overalls, carpenters wear beige. Manual workers wear blue and though, strictly speaking, bleach and solvents are not environmentally friendly, bricklayers and painters wear white.

Material possessions are also a pretty good indicator of status. That, and the height of your flag pole.

Wealth and status

Being average in Denmark is respectable, even desirable. Success is a solitary pleasure not to be publicly flaunted unless you're absolutely outrageous, in which case it's tolerated as an eccentricity and you can cruise in under the *Jante* radar. Snobbery about jobs is almost non-existent and most people can afford the everyday luxuries of life. Being ambitious and making money is fine, but sending your children to fee-paying schools (of which there are a handful in Denmark, modestly called Little Schools) is unnecessary. Outside Copenhagen it's considered bad form to buy privilege over and above what the State provides, and to stand out from the crowd in any way is considered a dangerous threat to the holy creeds of *hygge* and *Jante*. Wealthier Danes have a hard time getting rid of their money in a socially acceptable way.

> **Being average in Denmark is respectable, even desirable.**

The luxury tax on cars makes them dangerously high profile, but that still leaves clothes and perfume, a good hairdo and designer goods of all descriptions. Jewellery, amber (the precious stone of Denmark), furniture and household items are all acceptable, provided they are stylish in a Scandinavian way. But a fine line has to be trodden to avoid the Curse of *Jante*, not to mention the attentions of the taxman.

Snobbery does rear its head in Danish society,

though chiefly among the young. Woe betide the 14-year-old without the right designer clothes, trainers and mobile phone. This imported trend is a plague to parents, who complain to each other about the Danish youth of today over a cup of coffee poured from their new, German-designed, £100 coffee pot.

Manners & Behaviour

The Danes have confidently liberated themselves from the petty forms of etiquette and the residue of subservience to superiors that still pass for manners in other societies. They are not hamstrung by politeness or political correctness and are more likely to step in to deal with a potentially embarrassing situation than the English. When confronted with obnoxious lunatics, epilepsy attacks and the victims of street violence, the average Englishman will purse his lips like a prune and scurry across to the other side of the road. A Dane will steam in shamelessly and clear up the mess.

66 The Danes have confidently liberated themselves from petty forms of etiquette. 99

They don't say they are sorry. If a customer rings and asks to speak to Mr. Jensen, a Dane may simply reply 'Mr. Jensen is not in'. 'I'm sorry' doesn't come into it. He is not sorry. He is quite glad Mr. Jensen is out putting his skills to good use. Freedom of speech may be a core Danish value, but on the publication of a dozen controversial Muhammad cartoons it took a certain national newspaper, a world of astounded diplomats and dramatically flagging Middle Eastern exports to encourage Danes to express anything remotely approaching regret.

Danes can't be blamed however for the fact that the word 'please' simply does not exist in Danish. Children are taught to say '*Bede om*' ('ask/pray for') instead. For example, 'May I ask for another lollipop?' Either way, the answer is the same.

They say what they think about sex, politics, religion, everything. Small talk can assume monstrous

66 They will tell you frankly how much they earn per hour and whether or not they shave their armpits. 99

proportions. They will tell you frankly how much their mortgage is, how much they earn per hour and whether or not they shave their armpits. They will ask you equally frankly, 'Is it hot in here or is it just my menopause?', or, 'How old are you, Scarlett? You don't mind me calling you Scarlett, do you, Ms Johansson?'

They do not appreciate lateness. When they are invited to a formal social gathering at a specified time, they turn up strictly when invited, if not before. So someone who has invited a Danish acquaintance as a guest should not be stepping out of the shower at the appointed hour. With the exception of close friends and the young, it is considered impolite to keep others waiting. Anyone excusing themselves for being more than a few minutes late for a business meeting will be greeted with a droll 'It happens', the inference being that it may happen, but not to me.

Punctuality may also help explain what appears to be thoughtlessness. Doors are seldom held open for the person following behind and motorists hardly ever let other drivers join the stream of traffic. The feeling is that 'If they want to be where I am now, they should have got out of bed five seconds earlier.'

> **66 An average Dane can move at the speed of a striking cobra when an additional supermarket checkout opens. 99**

When making telephone calls, Danes politely begin by stating their name which means that instead of saying 'This is Mr. Skjoldbøl', a Dane says his or her full name and uses the impersonal form, e.g., 'It is Bent Skjoldbøl.' This leaves a foreigner on the other end wondering if it's a name or an injury.

Queuing is disliked. An average Dane can move at the speed of a striking cobra when an additional supermarket checkout opens. No-one bats an eyelid if someone beats other contenders to the conveyor belt. In Britain the person concerned would be strung up by his sausages, but not in Denmark.

The custom of removing footwear before entering the house has more to do with leaving heelmarks in wooden floorboards than anything else. At parties high heels are greeted with shocked silence. Firstly they are ergonomically questionable and, secondly, so many streets are composed of cobblestones or granite sets that you would be more likely to end up in A & E than at the party.

Toasting others

In Denmark spirits are raised collectively. At a meal with other people, rather than simply picking up your glass and drinking from it, it is customary to drink a *skål* (roughly translated as 'cheers'). *Skål* means 'bowl', which in Viking times was full of liquor and passed around the table. You had to yell 'Skål!' loudly to get a slurp.

Nowadays a *skål* entails picking up your glass, catching someone's eye, raising your glass to head height, waiting for anyone else

> **Rather than simply picking up your glass and drinking from it, it is customary to drink a *skål*.**

who wants to join in, looking round at all who are involved, raising the glass a couple of inches higher, and saying '*Skål*', before bringing the glass to your mouth. In reverse order, the glass is taken from the mouth and held head-high, everyone involved looks round at everyone else, smiles and nods approvingly, and the glass is replaced on the table, ready for the process to begin again.

It would be bad manners not to drink when so encouraged, and for a guest it is good manners to single out one's host and hostess and drink a *skål* with them, and with the people on either side, and the people opposite, and with anyone else who may have been previously omitted. A person can get pie-eyed in no time.

Greetings

Danes are not great social kissers. For most purposes a handshake will do. The frequency of handshaking in Denmark lies somewhere between the English, who do it once in a lifetime, and the French who shake hands whenever they have been out of the room. When something more than a handshake is required, Danes adopt a non-kissing embrace. There is no facial contact, just a dignified leaning together of the upper halves of the body, and maybe a mutual clapping on the

66 Danes are not great social kissers. For most purposes a handshake will do. 99

back. But – horror of horrors – the man hug is becoming ever more popular.

Third-party introductions are unheard of. At private gatherings, after handing over flowers, chocolates or wine to their hosts, Danes will go round and introduce themselves to everyone present. At this stage no conversation is struck up that will prevent the new arrivals from completing their tour of introduction.

This is very disconcerting for non-Danes as they assume that they are expected to remember everybody's name. In fact it's just a polite formality.

The custom can also cause problems for Danes attending functions abroad. If the host is busy, the Danish guest may simply walk through the door, stride up to a complete stranger in mid-mingle, grasp his hand and shake it vigorously while barking his own name. At the end of an evening, Danes will go round the guests again and take their leave. No slipping off unnoticed to enjoy the latest detective series without a plausible alibi.

> **66** No conversation is struck up that will prevent the new arrivals from completing their tour of introduction. **99**

When meeting friends, people cover themselves for any recent hospitality by saying '*Tak for sidst*' (Thank you for the last time). When meeting part of a family group it is usual to ask them to *Hils* (say hello to) the other members of the family. Originally it was customary to say, for example, '*Hils* Jens' or '*Hils* Karen' but naming the name is now optional. This is convenient when 'Say hello to your wife' is risky enough.

Forms of address

Despite the general lack of formality in Danish life, there is one area where some Danes retain an almost ceremonial correctness – they include a person's professional occupation before their name. When filling in forms, such as an application for a bank account, people state their occupation. This means that bank statements, future correspondence, etc., can then be addressed either to: '*Fr.* (Ms.) Karen Hansen' or *Biblioteks-assistent* Karen Hansen (Library Assistant Karen Hansen).

As her career progresses, Ms. Hansen must make sure to inform the bank when she becomes successively *Bibliotekar* (Librarian), *Overbibliotekar* (Senior Librarian), *Stadsbibliotekar* (Chief Librarian) and finally in retirement *Fhv. Stadsbibliotekar* (Former Chief Librarian Karen Hansen).

There are three possible reasons why this formality persists in an otherwise informal society. The first is that people train for so long to obtain their profession-al qualification that they identify strongly with their occupation and are proud of it. The second is that so many people are called Karen Hansen that something is needed to distinguish between Karen Hansen the library assistant, and Karen Hansen the sales consultant. The third reason is that Danes do this as a matter of habit, and have never thought not to.

66 So many people are called Karen Hansen that something is needed to distinguish between them. 99

The use of the formal 'you' – *De* for both singular and plural – has almost disappeared, though it still persists among the very old and in the most expensive shops and restaurants. It is also useful for taking the high ground when dealing with customer complaints.

Leisure & Pleasure

Time off

In spring, the most beautiful place to be is in a beech forest, striding through the carpet of white anemones with the sun shining through the fresh lime-green canopy. In summer, woodland clearings are perfect for sand-free picnics, and in autumn all you need is a basket to go scuffing about in the glorious gold, red, and russet leaves hunting for mushrooms.

As with other nations, foreign package-tour holidays are popular with Danes, but holidays at home still top the list, with a peculiarly Danish institution known as the summer house. These are found wherever there is a beach, sprouting like fungus around seaside villages. Sometimes there

66 With Danes, holidays at home still top the list, with a peculiarly Danish institution known as the summer house. 99

is a whole complex of them, with warrens of streets and skeletons of postmen who died trying to find their way out of the maze.

A typical summer house is made of wood to give the impression of ruggedness. It is a small affair, roughly the size of a two-roomed flat, with a garden to match. The majority were knocked up in the boom period of the early 1970s and were definitely not built to last. As they are only used for a few weeks each year this doesn't seem to matter that much to the owners, who potter around in a caricature of practical efficiency doing things with creosote and garden tools that they never have time to do at home.

> **❝ The Danes' clapboard buildings and love of bare floorboards could be said to reflect a hankering for the planking of the old Viking longships. ❞**

Danes who live in the city and have no garden or summer house may escape to soak up the sun with friends in a *kolonihave* – a cheerful allotment garden with a beautifully tended hut (a sort of Wendy-house for adults) – where the flag is flown when the owners are in residence.

Boating

The Danes have always been a seafaring people. Their clapboard buildings and love of bare floorboards in their houses and apartments could be said to reflect a hankering for the planking of the old Viking long-ships.

On any fine summer weekend day, with the sun shining and breezes blowing, the marinas will be packed with boats. There are hundreds of islands and harbours, and nowhere in Denmark is far from the sea.

Boats are immensely popular, but there is a distinction between 'boats' and 'boating', ownership being considerably more widespread than the activity. All through the summer, Danes with a real or imagined nautical bent will be found scrubbing and polishing their precious hulls, gazing jealously at the bigger vessels in the marina while sneering at the lesser ones. They may swap the suburban garden fence for the rails of a boat, but their values are the same.

> **There is a distinction between 'boats' and 'boating', ownership being considerably more widespread than the activity.**

For those who bravely put out to sea in their gleaming craft, sailing combines everything that Danes hold dear: fresh air, a pollution-free energy source, stylish but practical waterproof Helly Hansen clothing and the feeling of being part of a crew working in unison towards a common goal. Plus, the mast is comfortingly like a flag pole.

Dog-walking

Dog-owning in Denmark is taken seriously, and many owners attend training sessions. Everyone is good at time management, so dogs live life in the fast lane too, running alongside bicycles to get their exercise instead of being taken for walks. '*I snor*' ('on a lead') notices are common, but there are few other dog traces to be seen. The Danes were pioneers of the custom of dog owners taking plastic bags on dog walks, for doing what dog owners do with plastic bags on dog walks. Offending piles are sometimes highlighted with cocktail-stick flags if slip-ups occur, so owners get the point.

Cycling

Cycling is to the Danes what skiing is to the Norwegians and driving is to the Germans. Not to ride a bike in Denmark is a sure sign of eccentricity. Danes identify with their cycling sporting heroes because most of them use bicycles every day. Bicycles are not only the most *miljøvenlige* form of transport, but good for the *kondi* (from *kondition*, meaning 'fitness').

66 Not to ride a bike in Denmark is a sure sign of eccentricity. 99

Children start learning to ride a bike from around the age of four and they're on the road a couple of years later. A Danish company called Larry vs. Harry launched the Bullitt range of fast cargo bikes which are now sold all over the world.

Competition cycling is extremely popular. After Bjarne Riis became the first Dane to win the Tour de France, people everywhere ran out and painted his name in white paint on the road. They then raced off to buy themselves the essential gear, from water containers to shiny saddle-padded cycling shorts, before hopping on to their bikes to join the ranks of cycling fanatics. They can still be seen hurtling along Danish roads with their jersey pockets back to front for better aerodynamics.

Football

Danish football has two problems. One is that though there are some very fine Danish football players, most of the best ones play for foreign clubs, which pay better and achieve the goal of side-stepping the taxman. The other is that many leading Danish football clubs have names such as AB, FCK, AaB and OB, which sound more like Treasury bonds than anything to cheer for.

> **66 The greatest asset of Danish football, apart from some very good players, is the fans. 99**

The greatest asset of Danish football, apart from some very good players, is the fans. Abroad they behave with good humour and sporting enthusiasm and are known as *roligans* (from *rolig* meaning still or quiet). This may be because it is impossible to work up a blood-lust for a team called B93.

Denmark has never really returned to earth after winning the European Cup in 1992. Qualifying for the final brought the whole country to such a fever pitch that some Danish passengers actually managed to persuade the captain of a flight from Norway to Copenhagen to fly over the stadium while the game was in progress.

Quite a few schools allow important qualifying games to be shown, but some employers are less sympathetic. One manager who watched a World Cup match during his lunch hour was subsequently given the boot.

Winter Sports

There is only one genuine winter sport in Denmark. It is played early in the morning, against the clock, with small hand-held implements called car windscreen scrapers.

66 Winter lasts as long as the other three seasons put together. 99

The rest are summer sports played indoors. Handball, badminton, indoor tennis, indoor hockey – any excuse to join a club and have some fun during the long winter evenings. Consequently Denmark has produced a long string of male and female world and All-England Champions.

Winter lasts as long as the other three seasons put together. Not only is it long, it can be gloomy. In mid-winter it never gets entirely light (while in midsummer it never gets entirely dark). Though the temperature hovers about freezing point, Denmark does not have the requisite ice or snow-covered mountains for outdoor winter sports. There is always enough snow to inconvenience traffic and to bring shovelling householders out on to the pavements, but seldom enough for fun. When there is, everyone who can do so grabs a motley collection of skis and toboggans and heads for anything resembling a hill before the snow disappears. Though the highest point in Denmark is actually Yding Skovhøj at 173 metres, it is popularly believed that this honour belongs to Himmelbjerget, the ironically named 'Heaven Mountain'. Danes seem to have a low expectation of heaven because it is only 147 metres high, just twice the height of St. Peter's in Rome.

Amusement parks

Tivoli is a pleasure garden in the middle of Copenhagen. But it is not simply that: it is a magical part of the Danes' childhood experience.

By day it offers a garden bursting with flowers and sparkling with fountains, a lake with a full-sized galleon, cafés and restaurants, swings,

> 66 Tivoli is not simply a pleasure garden: it is a magical part of the Danes' childhood experience. 99

rides, roundabouts, and clowns – a place for senior citizens to sit having coffee and cakes, joined by shell-shocked parents recovering from the entrance fee. Together, they can watch small children eating candyfloss, wide-eyed with wonder. By night, it becomes a fairyland of glow lamps with a concert hall, the Tivoli Youth Guard (a children's marching band), a theatre for revues, acrobatic shows, a rock concert venue, an open-air pantomime with Harlequin and Columbine, ghost trains, big dippers, beer halls with communal singing, popcorn, ice cream, and fireworks.

Tivoli has been thriving since 1843, maintaining a balance between well-loved traditions and the latest in entertainment, between robust fun and simple enjoyment. Denmark also has the world's oldest operating amusement park. Dyrehavsbakken (Deer park hill), commonly known as Bakken (the hill), dates back to 1583. Bakken is the second most popular attraction in Denmark, after Tivoli. It's cheaper and more cheerful than Tivoli and it's a lovely for picnics on dry summer evenings.

66 Danes are Olympic drinkers – it even says so in *Hamlet*. 99

For Danes, amusement parks are the embodiment of innocent pleasure, where everyone can slip away for a while from the serious business of being adult.

Drinking & Eating

Danes are Olympic drinkers – it even says so in *Hamlet*. Alcohol can be bought without difficulty 24 hours a day, seven days a week, throughout Denmark

– even at petrol stations.

All Danish towns have cafés where people go to drink hot chocolate and enjoy a pastry while using the free WiFi and reading the free newspapers. In pubs, Danes can be seen playing backgammon and games with dice, generally for drinks.

The favoured traditional spirit is *snaps*, which is potato-based. Otherwise, Danes are partial to pretty much anything better than industrial turpentine. In the good old days it was common practice to start the day with a shot of snaps for fortification against a cold winter's morning (even in summer) and sink a few beers throughout the day at work. There would be more beers after work, a couple with supper and then a swift one or two later in the local bar. For adults, all that has changed now. These days, after-work drinking is usually restricted to Fridays.

Beer

What oil is to Texas, beer is to Denmark. Around half of the 600 million litres of Danish beer is exported annually – about 527 million billion pints.

Drinks are sold in bottles and cans and the deposit, which is not included in the price shown, can come as a shock. Trolleys full of empties for recycling purposes are trundled openly through shopping centres. No-one feels obliged to pretend that they have just had a party or cleared out their garage.

Full or empty, transporting crates is heavy work, especially on a bicycle, so cliques of hardcore Carlsberg connoisseurs often save themselves the trouble by disposing of the beer immediately outside supermarkets.

Apart from Carlsberg and Tuborg, there are many local brewers and each brewery has its supporters, almost as if it were a football team. The beers come in different strengths; some are very strong, especially the Export

66 Each brewery has its supporters, almost as if it were a football team. 99

beers which happily do not all get exported. Weaker (light) beers which have a low alcohol content are popularly known as 'cissies' beer'.

Carlsberg and Tuborg, though regarded as rivals, are owned by the same company and even come from the same brewery. In the old days the more academically or philanthropically minded drank their beer either in the cause of art or of science because Carlsberg was a great contributor to the arts and Tuborg to scientific research. Tuborg has now turned from science to the arts with the funding of Green concerts, so these days it's more a matter of taste.

Breweries bring out special beers every year at Easter and Christmas. University lecturers know all about 'P-day', the day when the *Påske* (Easter) beer hits the streets and students hit the pavements; and the launch of Tuborg's *'snebajer'* (snow beer) in November causes national celebration. On the appointed day, Danes everywhere wait impatiently as the seconds are counted down until the hour of its official release.

Snebajer beer coincides with the season of Christmas parties held by the vast majority of companies on a Friday afternoon, and followed by a weekend of alcohol-induced cold turkey. All manner of bad behaviour is tolerated if the transgressor is in his cups. In fact, not letting one's hair down at a party is to risk being called a spoilsport. However, Danes expect people to hold their drink, which is why they are so contemptuous of the Swedes whose alcoholic excesses

❝ All manner of bad behaviour is tolerated if the transgressor is in his cups. ❞

they consider to be beyond the pale. In one Carlsberg advertisement, a typical Swede had to agree not to urinate in a public place, make obscene gestures to Danish girls, be sick on the pavement or fall asleep on the bus to the ferry, before he was allowed to drink Danish beer.

The un-Danish pastry

In Denmark the 'Danish pastry' is known neither as Danish nor as pastry. These sinfully tempting creations were apparently introduced to Denmark in

1850 by Austrian bakers and are therefore called *wienerbrød* (Vienna bread).

Every baker's window is stuffed with these glazed confections, as well as cakes, tarts, rolls and biscuits. Each delicious treat has its own specific name, for example: snail, goose breast, frog snapper, gallop kringle, and one, which oozes custard, called a baker's bad eye. This may help to explain why a clever marketing executive somewhere cooked up the all-embracing term 'Danish pastry'.

Bacon

'Danish' bacon (along with the best quality meat) is produced almost entirely for the export market. The leanest thing about bacon in Denmark is the production process. Danes eat a lot of pork, some of it cured, but he who seeks bacon in Denmark may find himself offered a squarish slab of something dark and forbidding that is bacon in name only.

> **❝ Denmark has twice as many pigs as people and pig business is big business. ❞**

Denmark has twice as many pigs as people and pig business is big business. Thanks to their serious political clout, pig farmers remain immune to the siren call of environmental awareness. Danish pig farms are invisible in the countryside, tucked away more firmly than fat deposits at a modelling audition.

Typical meals

The best thing about breakfast is the freshly baked rolls. Even in the dead of winter on Sunday mornings the menfolk shrug on their overcoats and brave the elements on their way to the baker's and battle home with paper bags bursting with bread and sweet pastries for their families.

Standard fare at lunch is the open sandwich, *smørrebrød*, 'butter bread'. There is, however, precious little bread involved. What there is looks like a small square of doormat with the bristles shaved off. Made of rye (which stays fresh for much longer than white bread), it's the base for a vast variety of toppings: mild cheese with peppers, celery and grapes or walnuts; strong cheese with radishes; salted beef with horseradish and pickles; smoked eel with scrambled egg and watercress; pickled herring with hard-boiled egg; pickled herring with capers and raw onion rings; the outrageous '*stjerneskud*' (shooting star) – a mound of shrimps, mayonnaise, fried fish and slices of tropical fruit, garnished with dill and a twist of lemon... Hybrids include the '*klap sammen*' ('clapped together') with two pieces of bread like an English sandwich, but with a filling one can actually taste.

> **"Smørrebrød looks like a small square of doormat with the bristles shaved off."**

A popular *smørrebrød is dyrlægens natmad* (a *dyrlæge* is a veterinary surgeon and ('*natmag*' is liter-

51

ally 'night food'). This consists of liver pâté on sour-dough bread with a slice of salted meat crowned with a layer of meat jelly. No-one knows why such a dish is called a Vet's Supper. Outsiders might view it as more of a dog's breakfast.

The main meal of the day is eaten between 6 and 7 o'clock. It starts early and is dealt with efficiently, sandwiched between work, school, society meetings and other activities. Danes are fond of meat: sausage or pork meatballs are regular favourites, or roast pork. A traditional dish called *brændende kærlighed* (burning love) consists of crispy bacon pieces served in their own fat and poured over mashed potatoes. Vegetarians have a hard time. Even the larger supermarkets do not respond to their needs. They are more likely to come away from the frozen food cabinets with frostbite than a ready-made meal.

> **Guests generally linger until the official signal to depart arrives in the guise of *natmad* (literally 'night food').**

On special occasions, meals are allocated much longer. In fact, guests at large-scale parties generally linger until the official signal to depart arrives in the guise of *natmad*. By the time this snack is served, even the most enthusiastic hostess is glancing at the clock and itching to get the coffee stains off her pine table. If the guests don't get the hint she can try serving '*skrub af suppe*', which translates as 'push off soup'.

The rite of the cold table

The true heart of Danish culinary arts is not in any particular dish, but in the whole concept and execution of the cold table. The basic elements are: the bread, the *pålæg* (the things that are put on the bread), and the *tilbehør* (the accessories, or the things that are put on the things that are put on the bread). But you wouldn't dream of putting just anything with anything. The right *tilbehør* should be used with the right *pålæg*, and the right *pålæg* should be used with the right bread.

The dishes must also be taken in the right order: first the marinated herring, then the red herring and the herring in curry sauce, all of this on rye bread. (Herring, *sild*, is so popular that the same word is used for a tasty young lady.) Next come shrimps with mayonnaise on white bread. Then a little *gravad laks* with mustard sauce on white bread with caraway seeds.

> **❝ Food is eaten with the right accompaniments on the right plate with the right cutlery. ❞**

Meanwhile, beer has been served, and a *skål* has been drunk. Then a *snaps* is poured, a welcoming speech is made by the host, and a *snapse skål* is drunk. The used plates are taken out and clean plates brought in along with a warm dish, meatballs with cucumber salad, or a breaded fillet of plaice with Danish *remoulade* (a relish used with everything from fish to junk food).

All the time the food is eaten with the right accompaniments on the right plate with the right cutlery, an eye has to be kept open for the entrance of fresh dishes or the need to join in the drinking of a *skål*.

> **❝ Christmas is the major festival of the year, and Danish children believe that Father Christmas comes from Greenland. ❞**

Between mouthfuls, guests are expected to remember to compliment the chef. Then it's on through the prepared salads to the cheese, and a free market for making speeches and *skål*. Finally, after saying the obligatory '*Tak for mad*' (thanks for food), everyone retires from the table to drink coffee and cognac and fill in any remaining gaps with small cakes.

A well-executed cold table is a genuine piece of Danish heritage, where the guests are active performers in a shared ritual.

Customs & Traditions

Christmas

Christmas is the major festival of the year, and Danish children believe that Father Christmas comes from Greenland. Whole families go out into the woods to fell their own carefully chosen fir tree, and collect moss and natural treasures. They then use every scrap of glue, fabric, wool and imagination to turn beech nuts, egg boxes and anything else into troll-like creatures called *nisser*.

Each house has its own real *nisse* who lives all the year round out of sight in the attic. However these mischievous beings only become active in December. They play tricks, leave small advent presents in stockings, and generally remind the family below that *nisser* cause trouble if they don't get their portion of festive rice pudding (with a dollop of butter) the night before Christmas. For the entire month, a *nisse* programme glues children to the television and each day many are given *kalendar* gifts – sweets, pens, hair bobbles, keyrings – anything from the toyshop bargain buckets that will last out the day.

On Christmas Eve, before joining hands and circling the tree (hung with plaited paper hearts, and often lit with real candles), the family sit down to roast duck, roast potatoes and

> **A surprise almond is hidden in the pudding and the person who finds it can lay claim to a present, usually a marzipan pig.**

red cabbage, and plenty of it. Several helpings are passed around before the rice pudding is served – or more upmarket creamy *risalamande* – and hot cherry sauce. A surprise almond is hidden in the pudding and the person who finds it can lay claim to a present, usually a marzipan pig. Unenlightened foreign visitors have been known to eat the almond, unaware of its significance, thus forcing the rest of the company to work its way through the whole pudding in search of the elusive nut.

One custom that the Danes have made into something special is *Julefrokost*, the office Christmas lunch. Unlike the family party, this is an informal event. Games are played, songs are only sung if people want to (strangely enough they often do) and office flirtations are carried on rather more openly than before. After a respectable time-lapse, all manner of gross indecency is tolerated. However, since Denmark's proud shipbuilding industry capsized in '80s and '90s and the shipyards closed, the sight of 600 shipyard celebrants naked, fighting, and dancing on the tables at 3 o'clock in the afternoon is now a thing of the past.

Other celebrations

Danes ring in the New Year with a bang. Millennium celebrations saw many exceeding the 5 kilo limit per household on 'explosives'. Incredibly, given the combination of alcohol and gunpowder, few accidents occur – the only dangerously short fuses belong to neighbours who forget to sedate their cats, dogs or horses.

Fastelavn is held in early February. Once upon a time a barrel was hung from a rope, and inside the barrel was a cat; the young blades of the area would take it in turns to gallop past the barrel on horseback and give it a hearty passing thwack with a stout club. The man who hit it hard enough to emancipate the cat won the game.

These days the cat is a cut-out pasted on the barrel, and the local children take turns to hit it with a club; when the bottom falls out so do the sweets, enough not just for the 'winner' but for everyone – very Danish. The child who liberates the sweets is called the 'cat queen' (*kattedronning*), and the one who knocks down the last barrel stave is the *kattekonge* ('cat king'), complete with crowns. More importantly this is when children dress up. Television characters, monsters, fairy-tale heroes, the question is not

> **❝ With the ending of the blackout of World War II, someone lit a candle in a window. Each year since, many repeat this simple silent tribute. ❞**

'What do you want to be when you grow up?' it is 'What do you want to be for *Fastelavn*?' For children this is the day that dreams come true. For parents it can be a last-minute nightmare: Disney costumes sell out fast.

Danes still commemorate the ending of the Second World War in Denmark on 4th May 1945. That evening, with the ending of the blackout, someone lit a candle in a window and the idea spread like wildfire throughout the land. Each year since, on the same day, many repeat this simple silent tribute.

St. Hans Eve, the longest day of the year, is the time

when people build bonfires, preferably on the seashore. As the sun sinks, a traditional song is sung to two different melodies and the fires are lit in an attempt to keep the sun's flames alive, and stop the year turning to winter. The climax of the evening is when the homemade witch on top of the bonfire catches light and 'flies' off to the home of all witches, Brocken Mountain in Germany. It is a stirring sight to see a chain of bonfires stretching along the coast on a still summer's evening (rain notwithstanding), and to feel a sense of community with people all over the country who are doing the same thing. *Hygge* on a national scale.

Anniversaries

Silver weddings are celebrated in style. In rural areas all the neighbours fly the *Dannebrog*, and friends gather in the early morning at the home of the happy couple. A triumphal arch of branches is erected around their door, a group of top-hatted horn players appears, and the celebrants are surprised in their beds by a serenade played and sung outside their window. However, the happy couple should not be so surprised that they haven't organised a hearty breakfast for anyone who may turn up.

> **❝ The celebrants are surprised in their beds by a serenade played and sung outside their window. ❞**

Halfway to the silver wedding is the copper wedding, commemorated after twelve and a half years of marriage, and thus not on the relevant date at all. It is not certain whether Danes do this due to their love of celebration, or pessimism about the prospects of couples hanging on for another dozen years.

Employers celebrate when their employees have worked for them for a significant number of years. Local newspapers acknowledge those celebrating 'round' birthdays (ones with a 0 or even a 5), anniversaries and retirements with a section of toothy grins and embarrassing snap shots sent in by relatives and so-called friends. Ageing gracefully is not easy in the glare of such publicity.

> **66 Danish humour suffers from the handicap of the Danes' literal-mindedness. 99**

Sense of Humour

Danish humour suffers from the handicap of the Danes' literal-mindedness ('Can you play the violin?' 'I don't know, I've never tried.')

In Denmark, sarcasm and self-deprecation are likely to be misunderstood. No-one dares say they are better than anyone else, but no-one would say they were worse. The person who says 'My cakes always rise like an arthritic elephant' will be told quite earnestly 'That's not true. You made a very nice sponge cake for us the Easter before last.'

New Danish comedy tends to be character driven and rather coarse, with maximum cringe factor. Main characters have to appal the audience with their ignorance, stupidity and vanity. The national TV channels sometimes broadcast very rude material at peak viewing times, no doubt in the spirit of free speach.

Stand-up comedians abound, but biting political satire is not widespread as there is so little to bite on in Danish politics. Teasing is acceptable, as long as the object of the teasing consents, but really savage attacks, even on the rich and famous, are virtually non-existent. To take things so far is considered un-*hyggelig* and therefore frowned upon.

> **66 Biting political satire is not widespread as there is so little to bite on. 99**

Older Danes have a weakness for bare-cheeked slapstick. Dirch Passer was the archetypal buffoon. In his film comedy about national service, he rushes out of the barracks late for parade and his trousers fall down. People used to be carried out of the cinema weeping with laughter.

Humour of a more sophisticated and zany kind is also popular, being highly visual, witty and clownish, but where the 'victims' of the humour do not need the sympathy of the viewer, which enables the Danes to enjoy guilt-free laughter.

Classic Danish humour is whimsical, almost surrealistic. For example, Victor Borge's impeccable timing spanned classical music, cleverly-crafted comedy and even puns on punctuation. Another well-known exponent of this was Storm P., a comic whose cartoons are still in print. There is even a museum of his work. Here are some examples:

'Have you been punished before?'
'No, only afterwards.'

'One often thinks about something, which, on reflection, turns out to be... unthinkable.'

'What did the Doctor say?'
'He said I needed to take things easy. That makes me uneasy.'

And for the truly surrealistic:

'Do you like oysters?'
'Yes, with red cabbage.'
'I said, do you like oysters?'
'Yes, with red cabbage.'

Storm P. was famous for cartoons featuring tramps such as Sophocles and Pericles. One of these went:

Sophocles: 'Tell me, Pericles, when does a Tuborg taste best?' Pericles: 'Always!'

This caption became one of the most enduring advertisements for the product.

Humour in everyday life is low-key, perhaps because Danes don't go in for small talk with strangers. However, the misfortunes of those who bring down the Curse of *Jante*, the antics of the neighbourhood *særling* (eccentric – from *sær* meaning special) plus local gossip are always good for a few laughs. For example, a miser invested his fortune in building a large crayfish farm 15 miles from a colony of herons, a protected species in Denmark. Villagers would drive miles out of their way to catch a glimpse of the farmer brandishing his shotgun in impotent fury while herons waded serenely in his private lakes, picking off his life's savings one by one.

Systems

Getting about

Things work in Denmark. They work without a great bureaucratic superstructure and without bribery or obligatory tips. Taxis have notices saying a service charge is included in the price – though *drikkepenge* (drinking money) is accepted with a smile.

Buses and trains are frequent and bus tickets double as train tickets, but the zone system used for working out the charge is as unfathomable to tourists (and Danes) as Danish Niels Bohr's model of the atom. Motorways take you almost wherever you want to go, though you may not realise you have arrived because the names on street signs are so small they are hard to read from a moving vehicle.

With no domestic car production, the Danes are able to put a massive luxury tax on the purchase of motor vehicles without this being regarded as a protective tariff or damaging to Danish industry. On the contrary, the policy promotes employment because one in three vehicles on the road in Denmark is over 9 years old, skilfully kept going by the car servicing sector. It also keeps the bicycle trade riding high. Hundreds of thousands of people use bicycles as a primary means of getting about. Copenhagen was one of the first cities to operate a coin-in-the-slot bicycle scheme where you disconnect a bike from one stand, cycle around town and retrieve your coin when you put the bike back in another stand wherever you end up.

> **66 One in three vehicles on the road in Denmark is over ten years old. 99**

With roughly 40 domestic ferry routes linking the islands, all Danish families use them at one time or another. One of the pleasures of travelling to and fro has always been the opportunity to get out of the car or off the train and stretch your legs, breathe fresh, salty air, enjoy a snack, see who else may be on board, and generally slow down and relax.

The longest suspension bridge in Europe (at the time of its construction) now replaces a former 60-

minute ferry ride steaming across the Storebælt (Great Belt) between Zealand and Funen. After 10 years of financial difficulties, engineering problems and political wrangling, this magnificent 4-mile bridge-tunnel link was completed. It now takes tourists only 10 minutes to cross, but a whole lot longer to fathom the queuing system before buying a ticket.

The bridge to Sweden is another striking landmark and an astonishing feat of engineering. To avoid problems with low-flying aircraft at Copenhagen Airport, designers created a tunnel that leads to an artificial island where the bridge begins. Officially the bridge is named the Øresundsbron, a word that is half Danish and half Swedish. The Danes aren't really bothered about what it's called. Other than members of the sizeable Danish community who have chosen to live in the Swedish town of Malmö (a 20-minute commute from Copenhagen), what self-respecting Dane would want to go to Sweden anyway?

❝ Danish commerce has the concept of 'loyal competition'. Everyone has a living to make... ❞

Shops and shopping

Danish commerce has the concept of 'loyal competition'. Everyone has a living to make, and in the long run people will be losers if they try to take the bread out of someone else's mouth. A consequence of all this consensus is that the monopolies commission is kept busy and prices remain high. Not that it matters because you can get a reasonable price for whatever you buy when you sell it again via online sites like *The Blue Paper* and *Yellow and free* which offer everything second-hand that you can imagine – furniture, tractors, horses, cars, clothes, even maternity bras, and needless to say, scores of bikes are re-'cycled' every week.

Because the Danes believe in quality more than convenience, there are still many independent specialist shopkeepers. In an effort to

> **❝ Because the Danes believe in quality more than convenience, there are still many independent specialist shopkeepers. ❞**

compete with the superstores, they do what they're good at: they form an organisation, design a good logo, brainstorm a slogan (e.g., 'Covers everything' for an indoor shopping centre, or 'Best in the long run' for a street where the shops are strung out so far you need a new pair of shoes to walk the length of it), and then co-operate in groups to share costs of purchasing and marketing. As a result, though linked by the major chains, not every Danish high street looks like every other high street.

In addition to supermarkets there are occupation-based hypermarkets, for example one for teachers and another for caterers. There also two types of chemist – the *apotek* and the *materialist*. The *apotek* is really a pharmacist concentrating mostly on selling medicines. The *materialist* sells goods which, in Britain, would be spread between the chemist, the ironmonger, the garden centre and the pet shop. Here you can find alternative medicines, flea powder, fertiliser, loofahs, soap, shampoo, turpentine, sandals, and jars of *kopatte salve* (cow udder ointment), the remedy for (teats and) chapped hands.

The difference in the cost of living between Denmark and Germany, especially in essential products like booze and tobacco, tempts many Danes to chance the attentions of Customs and Excise. Border trade is worth millions of pounds a year. No matter that European regulations are evening out the differences,

> **66 At the *materialist* you can find flea powder, fertiliser, loofahs, sandals and jars of cow udder ointment. 99**

Danes still flock to the special supermarkets built for their custom that throng the German border area in south Jutland.

Thanks to EU legislation, smuggling is no longer the pensioner sport it once was (stuffing cigarettes down their trousers and decanting whisky into innocent-looking containers), though one elderly couple were caught bringing into Denmark a total of 800 litres of spirits and 30,000 cigarettes. They claimed in court that these were for 'private use' because they were saving up for the husband's 80th birthday party.

Education and training

Despite a great deal of evidence to the contrary, the Danes believe they have the highest educational standards in the world. This belief is based on the traditional length of university degree courses, and the thoroughness of vocational training.

School starts at the age of six, before which children are not encouraged to read or write (the attitude is: let kids play while they are young). As a result, and because many letters in the Danish alphabet are 'dual-action' or silent in spoken Danish, spelling is not a Danish forte. The Danes find this difficult to swallow, along with their glottal stops.

66 School starts at the age of six. The attitude is: let the kids play while they are young. 99

At the age of 16 or so, the more practically talented receive vocational training, and the more academically minded move up to a *gymnasium* (high school) – from which they 'graduate' with special colour-coded caps and a class trip on an open-topped lorry going from one parent's home (or homes, since the parents are likely to live apart) and crate of beer, to the next. For those who survive, university is next.

Until recently the average time taken to get a first degree was roughly ten years. This was because the minimum standard time was about six years, so students had to get jobs to support themselves while they studied, and thus took longer to complete the course. Because they took longer to complete the course they would start having families so they took longer still to complete the course. Even so, it has always taken a very long time to get a university degree – though Danes like to relate this to the depth of study rather than any slowness of progress.

Crime and punishment

The Danes are quintessentially a law-abiding people. Apart from the national sport of outwitting the tax-man, Denmark tops the list of countries within Europe which most dutifully enact domestic legislation to implement European laws. People even wait for the little green man at crossings.

> **66 Imprisonment in Denmark may appear to be a soft option, but it's hard to fault as it seems to work. 99**

Denmark is not as safe as it once was. Bikes have to be locked. Now and then in some areas rival gangs take pot shots at each other and the Danes are willing to pay dearly to preserve free speech, which puts them in the spotlight.

Imprisonment in Denmark is not intended to brutalise the prisoner. Treat him brutally, he will behave brutally, is the belief. Prisoners cook their own meals, wear their own clothes and can enjoy private family visits once a week. It may appear to be a soft option, but it's hard to fault as it seems to work.

Characteristically, in the case of the rejected suitor of a married female priest who consistently disrupted Sunday services by shouting, heckling and drinking, the local police adopted a softly-softly preventive approach, apprehending the culprit on the way to the church and detaining him at the station until after the final Amen.

Culture

Design

Danish design is famed for its lightness and elegance. Large wooden coffee tables seem to float on thin air and flights of stairs appear to take flight. Designer *brugskunst* (the art of the usable) fetches high prices in furniture, lighting, textiles, silverware, porcelain, and so forth. Some objects are such classics of design and form that newly-qualified Danish furniture designers complain of manufacturers

> **❝ Large wooden coffee tables seem to float on thin air and flights of stairs appear to take flight. ❞**

not being interested in trying new ideas. The furniture of Arne Jacobsen and the lamps of Poul Henningsen (both distinguished architects) are still produced and exported in large quantities even though these designs date from the early 1950s. Erik Jørgensen's sofas and Hans Wegner's wooden chairs have been sought after for decades, as have Nanna Ditzel's ring chairs –

though it seems Danish designers would sometimes rather spend time designing their furniture than sitting back on it and relaxing. Which could explain why comfort occasionally takes a back seat.

In the hands of a Dane even the definition of the humble kitchen tap is open to interpretation. These sculptures of 'Anguish in Stainless Steel' are often a combination of chunky tubes, spouts and angled levers which have to be pushed, pulled, twisted or swivelled with care to avoid an unexpected jet of boiling or freezing water.

> **66 Danish architects have been responsible for beautiful modern buildings all over the world. All round Denmark, too. 99**

Timeless designs include the label on the Carlsberg bottle, post boxes, and Georg Jensen silverware. There are Royal Copenhagen designs for china dating back to the 18th century. Denmark, however, is no sterile design museum and there is constant renewal: you have only to think of the style and skills involved in producing the best-known consumer goods, such as sound systems and televisions by Bang & Olufsen who introduced the concept of industrial design to home electronics.

Danish architects have been responsible for beautiful modern buildings all over the world. The Sydney Opera House by Jørn Utzon is probably the most famous, but contemporary architects such as BIG and Dorte Mandrup are firmly established global names.

All round Denmark, too, there are well-designed public buildings – concert halls, railway stations, libraries and town halls. Unfortunately, design skills are less frequently applied to domestic architecture and Denmark has its share of dreary blocks of flats and rows of ugly bungalows. Being born Danish does not guarantee impeccable taste.

Radio and television

Danish radio stations are very good. DR is Denmark's oldest and largest media enterprise. However the flagship company almost ran aground in its attempt to relocate to the vast DR-Byen complex. The budget overspending scandal even caused waves in the Danish parliament, where a bail-out was debated. Now the major threat facing Danish television is the tidal wave of reality programmes.

> **❝ Cable television has an effect on the language skills and cultural orientation of the different regions. ❞**

Many people have turned to cable television as an alternative source of entertainment. Even those TV sets not specially hooked up can receive Swedish programmes in the east of the country and German programmes in the south. This has an effect on the language skills and cultural orientation of the different regions. People in the east understand Swedish, whereas southern Jutlanders speak excellent

German having being brought up on a diet of foreign films dubbed in German – '*Ich heisse Bond. James Bond.*'

Judging by programming schedules, Danes enjoy live audience debates. The same subjects are bandied about week after week (welfare, immigrants, television violence, tax), starting at the same starting point and finishing in mid-sentence without reaching a specific outcome.

> **66 Danes enjoy live television debates – starting at the same point and finishing in mid-sentence without reaching a specific outcome. 99**

Classic British detectives such as Morse, Barnaby and Frost are warmly received in Denmark, as are the newer American series like *CSI*. The home-grown high-calibre Danish whodunnit *The Killing* ('The Crime' in Danish), was instrumental in putting Danish TV drama on the international map. Despite subtitles, *The Killing* glued British viewers to their TV screens with its dark intrigue and taciturn heroine in her *hyggelige* Faroese sweaters.

Borgen, a Danish TV drama series about a female Prime Minister proved even more popular. These big budget, flagship Danish productions have the whole country following them, and for weeks on end monopolise the headlines. More minor stories like discovering life on Mars are relegated to the inside pages.

Literature

Children all over the world have delighted in the tales of Hans Christian Andersen. This strange, shy man with his enchanting fairy tales and stories including *The Ugly Duckling*, *Thumbelina*, *The Princess and the Pea*, *The Snow Queen*, *The Emperor's New Clothes* and *The Nightingale* put Denmark on the literary map, and his fame contributes to huge sums spent by tourists. The sculpture of his *Little Mermaid* is the only landmark (suitably modest in size) for which Denmark is famous.

Apart from Hans Christian Andersen, whose thinking is easy to understand but whose writing is inelegant, the most

> **For the Danes, culture is a way of shedding the modern world and retracing their roots.**

famous Danish writer is Søren Kierkegaard, whose writing is elegant but whose thinking is difficult to understand. Kierkegaard is credited with (or blamed for) being the founder of existentialism; in his lifetime hardly anyone read his works, and those who did thought he was a nuisance, but his influence reached far beyond the borders of Denmark.

Three Danish authors have won the Nobel prize for their literary achievements: Henrik Pontoppidan and Karl Adolph Gjellerup (both 1917), and Johannes V. Jensen (1944), though they are little known outside Denmark. More recently Inger Christensen (*It*) and Peter Peter Høeg (*Miss Smilla's Sense of Snow*) reached a global audience.

For the Danes, culture is a way of shedding the modern world and retracing their roots. All Danes are inveterate nature lovers. They cultivate an almost masochistic feeling of insignificance coupled with awe at nature's power and the forces of life. Danish literature is full of examples of characters trying to come to terms with man's essential loneliness and unimportance.

> **Danish literature is full of examples of characters trying to come to terms with man's essential loneliness and unimportance.**

Tom Kristensen's 1930 classic *Hærværk* (*Havoc*), is the story of a once politically active journalist who deliberately sets out to destroy himself and his new respectable life through drink and infidelity.

In Pontoppidan's greatest work, *Lykke Per*, an unrealistically ambitious priest's son from a country district is given the chance to realise his aims and achieve greatness. Just when success and happiness are in his grasp he turns his back on them and embraces failure and unhappiness, realising that this is what fate ordained for him; this is how he must be true to his innermost self. It is as if Pontoppidan turns the story of the *Ugly Duckling* on its head; if you are born a duck you can dream about being a swan, but you are still a duck.

Karen Blixen's writing was less philosophically motivated, though she is nevertheless seen as a feminist heroine because of her struggle to overcome the affliction of a wastrel husband who spent her money and infected her with syphilis before abandoning her. Confusingly, she wrote under the various names of Karen Blixen, Isak Dinesen and Pierre Andrézel. But now she is to be eternally remembered as Meryl Streep in *Out of Africa*.

The performing arts

The nation competes in the première league in the world of ballet. The Royal Danish Ballet is famous for being the home of the 19th-century choreographer, August Bournonville, whose ballets include the immortal *La Sylphide*.

The oldest film company in the world, Nordisk Films, (founded in 1905) is Danish. A pair of Danish film comedians called Lighthouse and Trailer (on account of one being tall and thin and the other being short and round) were world famous until the talkies came along.

> **66 Blixen wrote under various names. But now she is to be eternally remembered as Meryl Streep in *Out of Africa*. 99**

Working against the disadvantage of having only a small market for films in their own language, a number of Danish film-makers have nevertheless had resounding international success. Dogma 95 was an avant-garde film-making movement started by Danish directors Thomas Vinterberg and Lars von Trier, which sought to make film-making more accessible by stripping the creative and production process down to a minimum. Von Trier is famous for films like *Breaking the Waves, Dancer in the Dark, Dogville, Antichrist* and *Melancholia.*

The name of Carl Th. Dreyer is known to a growing circle of film aficionados. He produced films which were full of doom and symbolism, and, working in the medium of black and white, was particularly skilful in his use of the black.

A unique form of entertainment is the *revy* (revue). In the summer, professional and amateur actors,

> **66 Nielsen's symphonies have a vigour which is strangely at odds with the Dane's equitable temperament. 99**

singers and entertainers in all provincial towns put on entertainments that are local, topical, amusing and musical. The audience delights in having things said and sung about their own community, and local dignitaries are treated with anything but dignity. It is a bit like pantomime except that the jokes, like the Dame's padded attributes, are well over the heads of any children present.

Hans Christian Lumbye has been called the Strauss of the North. His bubbly *Champagne Galop* was composed to celebrate Tivoli's second birthday in 1845. Another great figure of Danish music is Carl Nielsen. Unlike his contemporary, Sibelius, whose works express and embody the Finnish national spirit, Nielsen's symphonies are distinctive but not nationalistic; they have a vigour which is strangely at odds with the Danes' equable temperament and the quiet Danish landscape.

He also wrote many songs, and set Danish poems to music. These are lyrical and tuneful, often expressing a love of the countryside, and have become part of the national heritage. *The Danish Song*, a Neilsen composition for a poem by Kai Hoffmann (first performed in 1926), echoes these sentiments:

> The Danish song is a young blonde girl who is humming in Denmark's house.
> She is the child of the sea-blue kingdom, where beech trees listen to the foaming waves.

Painters

At the turn of the 20th century, the town of Skagen on the northern tip of Jutland was home to a school of painters. Its clear skies, and pale gold and platinum sands inspired artists like P.S. Krøyer, Michael and Anna Ancher, L.A. Ring, and others not necessarily working in Skagen, like Hammershøi and J.F. Willumsen, who developed a technique for showing how light plays on water and in the air. Constantly reproduced on greetings cards, their images of seashores and sunlight, family parties, domestic interiors, fishermen and country workers are invested with dignity enriched by affection. In rather the same way as some 17th-century Dutch painters celebrated their everyday life, they made the ordinary look beautiful, and full-length petticoats remain whiter than white, even after long strolls along the shore.

Business & Commerce

The guild system

The whole of Danish business life is marked by the residual spirit of the guild system. Vocational training is still required for most jobs. This applies not only to doctors, dentists and lawyers, but to all kinds of trades.

> 66 The guild system means Denmark is still a nation of experts. 99

In order to change an electric light socket, you must be a fully trained electric light socket changer. Your training as an electric light socket changer will be very thorough, including a review of the history of electric light sockets, and, of course, light bulbs; the variety of designs and purposes of electric light sockets will be considered, as well as their social role, and the possible consequences of poorly-fitted sockets. Once you are a certified electric light socket changer, you will become a member of the electric light socket changers' union and get a job, or at the very least, become a member of that union's publicly funded unemployment scheme.

The guild system is reinforced by the way in which unemployment pay is administered. For instance, the Hairdresser and Cosmetic Union administers the unemployment fund for hairdressers and beauticians. A hairdresser may not be obliged to join the union, but if he wants unemployment insurance, for which he has already largely paid through his taxes, he has to subscribe for it through the union's unemployment scheme.

This leads to inflexibility in the labour market. If a hairdresser loses his job and seeks work as a window dresser, he must leave the hairdresser's unemployment fund and put at risk his being able to get work again as a hairdresser, despite his long years of training. Thus the modern Dane suffers from the new feudalism, bound to his house by debt and to his trade by the unemployment and qualification schemes.

On the positive side, the guild system means Denmark is still a nation of experts. It may cost you a fortune to have a light socket changed, but you'll get a beautiful job.

Service and manufacturing

With no raw materials of their own, the Danes have become adept at carving themselves a niche in the international chain of production. Danish companies specialise in quality, research, efficiency, know-how and consultancy. These they 'implement' with a lot of team spirit and all the latest management techniques.

Amazingly for its size, Denmark has a number of very high-profile multi-national companies: Bang & Olufsen, of course, Carlsberg, LEGO (still massive after all these years of electronic toys), Vestas, Maersk – the oil, shipping and transport giant – Arla selling dairy products, and Novo Nordisk, a major pharmaceutical concern specialising in medicine and gene-spliced products. The Danes' strong point seems to be to offer high-quality products that others want to buy.

> **The Danes' strong point seems to be to offer high-quality products that others want to buy.**

They have managed to grab a sizeable piece of the action in some unexpected areas, like marine electronics and insulin (which is linked to pig farming), pipeline assembly and container storage facilities. The biggest industrial sector is agriculture, together with associated food-processing industries like bacon, butter and beer. The leading manufacturer of potato crisps is also the leading distiller of *snaps*, both being the product of the humble spud. Farming may now be capital intensive but the autumn school half-term is still referred to as the 'potato holiday', from the days when children were wanted in the fields to bring in the harvest.

The most characteristic Danish workplace is small, run by highly trained, self-employed people making products such as chocolate manufacturing machinery, pumps and compressors, furniture, boats, medical equipment and porcelain.

A high proportion of the Danish workforce is employed in the service sector. Quite

66 In many fields being smart is a state of mind, not of clothing. 99

apart from the usual service industries, like banks, transport, utilities, etc., this sector is swollen by the number of carers employed. Mr. Hansen goes out to work to look after Mrs. Jensen's mother in an old people's daycare centre. To be able to go out to work, Mr. Hansen has to leave his children in a daycare centre. Mrs. Jensen takes her mother to the old people's daycare centre on her way to work, which consists of looking after Mr. Hansen's children at the children's care centre. Job rotation in full swing.

In the office

In many fields being smart is a state of mind, not of clothing. Wearing a suit to the office is rarely required unless executives from a foreign parent company are likely to drop in. Feeling comfortable and at ease is all part of creating a *hyggelig* atmosphere in which to conduct a productive meeting. This overt friendliness can be misunderstood. Danes don't exactly roll up their sleeves and kick off their shoes, but they seem to be quick to get their feet under the table. They mix business and pleasure, sometimes telling appalling jokes to break the ice.

❝ The workload is extreme – Danes need their minimum five weeks' holiday a year. ❞

There are no long business lunches: with flexi-time, lunch hours are often lunch half-hours. Middle managers join the canteen queue with everyone else or sit in the lunch room enjoying their *madpakke* (packed lunch) and a lager or *Danskvand* (Danish mineral water) – anything with *dansk* in its name has to be good.

Competitors are often acquaintances, for in a small country like Denmark it is likely that one manager has been at business school with another, or that they have been colleagues, or can expect to become so. Bosses will listen to the views of people lower down the hierarchical ladder because they believe them to be knowledgeable about their own sphere.

Danish employers demand a great deal from their employees but they also respect them and treat them accordingly. Promotion is performance-based and the workload is extreme – they need their minimum five weeks' holiday a year. Firms with multi-national clients are expected to be on call 24 hours a day, which means that if the phone rings from Hong Kong at 3.30 in the morning, you jump out of bed, drive to the office and get cracking.

Government

The Queen

Denmark is a constitutional monarchy – one of those which are sometimes quaintly described as a 'bicycle monarchy'. There is, however, nothing of the free-wheeler about the Danish Queen.

Margrethe, known affectionately as Daisy, is looked up to not just because she is tall, but because she is multi-talented. In addition to costume design for television theatre and scenery for ballet, she is an accomplished linguist and artist: the Danish publication of Simone de Beauvoir's *All Humans are Mortal* is her translation and her illustrations grace a special edition of *The Lord of The Rings*. She has also designed commemorative postage stamps, and created

> **66** Queen Margrethe, known affectionately as Daisy, is looked up to not just because she is tall, but because she is multi-talented. **99**

needlework patterns that anyone can buy and sew. Her only self-confessed failing is that she smokes, for which the populace love her even more.

Rain or shine, on her birthday hordes of flag-waving Danes congregate beneath her bedroom window to shout 'Queen, Queen come out! Or we won't go home!' – and she does, despite the absence of the word 'please'.

Political parties

The Danish voter has a plethora of political parties to choose from since any party getting 2% or more of the popular vote is assured parliamentary representation. In fact, a negative parliamentarism applies since the government does not need a majority behind it at all times, but must never have a majority against it (at least not in important matters).

> 66 In Danish politics, co-operation and self-interest are close cousins. 99

There are so many parties in Parliament (*Folketing*) that no party can ever rule without the support of others, and no party is ever without hope of having a share of government. The Government is therefore always a coalition government and usually, even as a coalition, it runs the country with a minority in Parliament. Thus no politician can ever be too rude about another politician, whatever his views, as he never knows when he will need the other's support. In Danish politics, co-operation and self-interest are close cousins.

It requires a certain dedication to vote in Denmark. Party names do not necessarily reflect their positions on the political spectrum. *Venstre* ('Left'), the Liberals, is a party of the right, while *Venstresocialisterne* (Left Socialists) are to the left of the Social Democrats, which puts the latter somewhere near the centre. The Liberal Alliance party is a centre-right party and

Radikale Venstre (Radical Left) is neither radical nor left, but so far to the middle it is said that their standard response to political proposals from other parties is: 'We're neither for nor against. On the contrary!' However, all governments pursue a mainly Social Democratic policy, whichever party is in office. An ex-prime minister once said that the trouble with the Danes is that they 'Work black, eat green and vote red'.

The Green Party's lack of progress in Denmark may seem strange in such an environmentally-friendly country. But the widespread consensus

> **66 An ex-prime minister once said that the trouble with the Danes is that they 'Work black, eat green and vote red'. 99**

on green issues across the political spectrum means that people do not need to support the Green Party to get mainstream issues addressed.

Denmark's most right-wing parliamentary political party is *Dansk Folkeparti* (Danish People's Party) with its clearly anti-immigration stance. The most left-wing parliamentary party is *Enhedslisten* (Red-Green Alliance), which is a socialist, communist and green party dedicated to the creation of a classless society.

A professional comedian called Jacob Haugaard was once voted into parliament with his one-man Party for Work-Shy Elements. One of his election promises was to provide a following wind on cycle paths.

Language

Danish is not a mellifluous language (as is, say, Italian), but it is economical. Why invent a new word when two old ones are perfectly adequate? For example, direct translations give: the dust sucker (vacuum cleaner), swine meat (pork), beating meat (stewing beef), body burning (cremation), flying machine (aeroplane) and breast wart (nipple). Words, like everything else, are recycled where possible: *hej* means hello, *hej, hej* means goodbye. The verb *at lide* can mean to suffer or to like. *Fyr* means fire, pine or young man. *Brud* means rupture, bride or weasel. Listeners have to pay attention to context and tone of voice if misunderstandings are to be avoided. Perhaps this is why Denmark has a 40% share of the global market for hearing aids.

> **66 Danish is not a mellifluous language, but it is economical. Words, like everything else, are recycled where possible. 99**

Danes, Norwegians and Swedes are tuned to each other's languages and can converse in their native tongues, though Danish and Norwegian sound very different. It has been observed that people in hilly countries speak with up-and-down sing-song accents. People in flat countries speak with flat accents. Denmark is a flat country.

There is no system of phonetic notation that can do

justice to spoken Danish. The consonants are often so softly enunciated as to be undetectable except to the trained ear, while the language possesses vowels that require the speaker to make noises that would be inadmissible in polite society in any other civilised country. Then there's the 'r'. The Italians and Scots roll their 'r's at the tip of their tongues; the German guttural 'r' is pronounced from the back of the throat.

The Danish 'r' has to be fetched from deep below the tonsils, and requires special muscles.

> **66 The Danish 'r' has to be fetched from deep below the tonsils, and requires special muscles. 99**

A knowledge of the Danish alphabet may seem esoteric, but it can be helpful to know, when using a dictionary, telephone directory or street map index, that v and w may appear together, aa is the same as å, and æ, ø and å are at the end of the alphabet. Anyone looking for Aabenraa at the start of a list will be driven round the bend.

When meeting foreigners attempting to speak their language most Danes adopt one of two strategies. They either begin glancing at their watches mid-sentence and then switch to English, or they persevere, fearing their language, like their golden coastlines, will otherwise ultimately be eroded and swamped. All take solace from the fact that Danish is so unspeakably difficult to pronounce that no foreigner can make it sound worse.

The Authors

Helen Dyrbye (née Pearce) grew up in Ormesby – a place of Viking origin with a name meaning worms' village – on the east coast of England. Her career as PR assistant for the Scout Association was diverted by marriage and relocation to Denmark where, after two years of glottal stopping and starting, she began her own English language consultancy. She now specialises in translating Danish texts of all kinds into reader-friendly English and writes a Kids' Corner column for *The Copenhagen Post*.

A remarried mother with three lovely sons, she believes herself pretty well integrated into Danish society. However she is still hopeless at combining the flamboyance of Danish open sandwiches with the practical limitations of packed lunch boxes. And despite the earnest efforts of various Danes to persuade her, she remains unconvinced by the idea that Danish longships contained peace-loving settlers who were kind enough to give the English natives a language.

Steven Harris was working for a multi-national in Brussels when he was moved to Copenhagen for 12 months' 'rotational' training. He went on rotating in Denmark for ten years. He knew he had mastered

Danish when people stopped telling him how well he spoke it.

A lawyer-linguist, he now lives in England with his Danish wife and three children, and works from home translating law books, articles, theses and other texts from Danish into English. Though retirement is tempting, he finds this occupation too satisfying to relinquish.

Thomas Golzen was born and brought up in London. He went to Denmark to work as a professional musician for three months in 1987, and never left.

After much travelling and a bewildering array of emergency jobs he settled in Copenhagen, where he still lives with his Danish partner and their three children. A graduate from the National Danish Film School, he is a freelance screenwriter and partner in a Danish advertising agency called Recognition. He also enjoys earning an occasional extra sixpence by twanging the guitar in his band, The Luminous Blue Variables.

The Italians

Generally speaking, the Italians tend to look on the bright side of life – a positive outlook aptly illustrated by their touching salutation: 'May the saddest days of your future be the happiest days of your past.'

The Greeks

Greeks exhibit an extreme passion for freedom of choice – which has turned law circumvention into an art and has made them incapable of comprehending words like 'discipline', 'co-ordination' or 'system'.

The French

It is the passion for matters of the intellect that makes the French natural philosophers. There is not a farmer, fisherman, waiter, car-worker, shop assistant or housewife who isn't a closet Descartes or Diderot, a Saint-Simon or Sartre.

The Americans

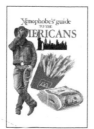

Winning is central to the American psyche. As American football coach Vince Lombardi put it, 'Winning isn't everything. It's the only thing.' Virtually every event in American life is structured so that one party wins.

The Estonians

Estonians are as sparing with material things as they are with their emotions. They will use five spoonfuls of coffee to make six cups, stand up in the bus to save wear on the seat of trousers, and divide a one-ply serviette in two.

The English

Tradition, to the English, represents continuity, which must be preserved at all costs. It gives them a sense of permanence in an age of change. Like a well-worn jersey with holes in the sleeves, it's the comfort of the familiar.

Xenophobe's®
guides

Available as printed books and e-books:

Xenophobe's®
lingo learners

Xenophobe's Guides